"What a fabulous and fantastic gift to yourself, to your relationship with Christ, to your friendships or family circle, and to your future! *Tethered Trust* is biblical, approachable, practical, and life-giving!"

—**Pam Farrel**, author of 60 books, including the coauthored *Discovering Wisdom in Proverbs* and *Discovering Hope in Psalms*

"What a relief! Becky Harling's *Tethered Trust* offers us an invitation to work through our trials in community and friendship. Her loving and confident voice points us to God's trustworthiness, and her meaningful guidebook helps women bond when they need it most!"

—**Amber Lia**, best-selling author of *Food Triggers* and coauthor of *Triggers*

"Living in our fast-paced society makes it difficult to forge meaningful and lasting relationships, but *Tethered Trust* offers a solution to address the problem. Its unique format invites readers into a deeper friendship with Jesus through understanding His names and their relevance to everyday life while drawing readers into deeper relationships with one another. I love how the author weaves Scripture, anecdotes, and reflection questions together to encourage honest engagement—a key to meaningful relationships with both Jesus and others."

—**Grace Fox**, codirector of International Messengers Canada, Bible teacher, podcaster, and author of 14 books, including *Names of God*

"There is no one I would rather learn about trust from than Becky Harling. There is no one I would rather learn about Jesus from than Becky Harling. Becky's faith is unshakable—she daily lives what she writes about. I have seen her trust God through unbelievably hard times, and she has modeled an uncompromising faith in the Savior's love. In her new book, *Tethered Trust*, Becky invites us to keep our eyes and our heart tethered to the One who never changes. I'm in! Are you?"

—**Carol Burton McLeod**, Bible teacher, podcaster, blogger, and best-selling author of *Meanwhile* and *Rooms of a Mother's Heart*

"In a world where women are lonelier than they've ever been, *Tethered Trust* is a gift beyond price. Author Becky Harling has provided a fun and biblically sound resource for nurturing current friendships and developing new ones. This is a book I'll recommend to my friends and use in my own personal small groups!"

—**Edie Melson**, director, Blue Ridge Mountains Christian Writers Conference

"Despite the demands of a busy life, it is crucial to carve out moments to cultivate our spiritual well-being. Becky's new book is an exceptional tool that enables girlfriends to strengthen their bond with one another while developing stronger individual relationships with God. *Tethered Trust* has many admirable qualities, but the 'Personal Consideration' section stands out as my favorite. In this section, amid the camaraderie of friends, there exists a quiet intimacy that is solely shared between you and God. Life is about connections, and just as we connect with each other, this book allows us to establish a connection with God. The book is reader-friendly with clear instructions in the 'What's Involved?' section on how to maximize its benefits."

—**Evelyn Johnson-Taylor**, PhD, Christian author and theology professor

Other Books by Becky Harling

Rooted Joy
Our Father
The Extraordinary Power of Praise
How to Listen So Your Kids Will Talk
Listen Well, Lead Better
Psalms for the Anxious Heart
Who Do You Say That I Am
How to Listen So People Will Talk
The 30-Day Praise Challenge for Parents
The 30-Day Praise Challenge
Freedom from Performing
Rewriting Your Emotional Script

Your Connection to a Name
Like No Other

Tethered

Trust

A GIRLFRIEND GATHERING STUDY OF ISAIAH 9:6

BECKY HARLING

IRON
STREAM

Birmingham, Alabama

Tethered Trust

Iron Stream
An imprint of Iron Stream Media
100 Missionary Ridge
Birmingham, AL 35242
IronStreamMedia.com

Library of Congress Control Number: 2023944047

Cover design by Jonathan Lewis / Jonlin Creative

ISBN: 978-1-56309-682-2 (paperback)

ISBN: 978-1-56309-683-9 (eBook)

1 2 3 4 5—28 27 26 25 24

This book is dedicated to my dear friend Keri Spring.

Keri, you have modeled for so many of us what it looks like to practice tethered trust.

May you continue to rest secure in God's faithfulness.

I love and appreciate you!

CONTENTS

PREFACE

Welcome, friends! *Tethered Trust* is the second book in the Girlfriend Gathering series and has been created to help you cultivate deeper trust in God. Each short book in the Girlfriend Gathering series has been developed for you to complete with a group of close friends with whom you can be authentic and vulnerable. You can use the material as a resource for a girlfriend retreat or as a short four-week Bible study.

Trust is a wonky concept. Right?! Is it a choice or a feeling? You might wonder, *What do I do when I want to trust God, but I just can't quite get there? Or, what about the times when I don't feel relaxed in God's presence, and yet I need His help? What then?* These are all questions we're going to dive into together in this short study of Isaiah 9:6.

Having a tight-knit community of friends with whom we can be authentically honest about our faith struggles will help us in our journey of trust. In addition to having a group who can help us process our feelings, our friends can help hold up our faith when we feel weak. And, the truth is, the transition from fear to faith usually happens best in community. So, gather your friends and dive in.

Before we get started, let me explain what's going to be involved.

What's Involved?

Tethered Trust is a study of Isaiah 9:6 and the four names of Christ that are listed there. Each session will include:

Exploration

This section will invite you to read certain passages of Scripture out loud. Then, you'll look for and have a conversation about the specific truths and meaning found in the passage.

Reflection

This section is divided into two parts.

- **Group Reflection: Let's Get Real!** These questions are designed to prompt you to share your thoughts, feelings, and struggles authentically with one another. Only as we become vulnerable are we able to truly experience transformation.
- **Personal Consideration.** In this section, each person is encouraged to spend time alone with God silently for at least twenty minutes to reflect on the questions given.

Application

- **Invitation.** In this section, you'll reflect on the question, How is God inviting me to respond?
- **Listen.** Each session will include a worship song for you and your girlfriends to listen to that will prompt your praise.
- **Suggested Girlfriend Activities.** This section will include suggested activities that will encourage your connectedness as friends.
- **Prayer Time.** During this time, you'll be invited to pray with and for one another. Nothing builds strong friendships quite like prayer.

- **Practical Tips.** This section will include practical tips related to the study.
- **Additional Scripture Passages.** Part of each session will include additional Scripture passages. You can look at these together and share what stands out to you, or you can save them to reflect on after your gathering.
- **Blessing.** At the end of each session, you will find a written blessing. Have one person read the blessing over your group.

A seven-day devotional plan is included at the end of the study so that you can continue the connection you've experienced. Each of you will complete the devotional plan independently, but you can stay in touch with one another and share what you are learning each day.

Before we get started, let me gently remind you of Girlfriend Gathering etiquette.

Girlfriend Gathering Etiquette
- Listen attentively.
- Keep all discussions confidential.
- Refrain from giving advice unless you are asked.
- Empathize with the feelings of your friends.
- Learn to ask thoughtful questions.
- Pray for your friends consistently.

Friends, as you gather and begin the journey to deeper trust, know that I am praying for you and cheering you on. As you seek to understand Jesus more deeply and lean into your community more fully, I am confident that the Holy Spirit will increase your faith.

Blessings and Joy,
Becky Harling

INTRODUCTION

Trust is not a passive state of mind. It is a vigorous act of the soul by which we choose to lay hold on the promises of God and cling to them despite the adversity that at times seeks to overwhelm us.

—Jerry Bridges

One of the dreams my husband, Steve, has had for a long time is to go skydiving. (I don't share that dream at all!) He was all excited when he discovered that an officer in the Air Force would be willing to take him up and teach him how to jump. However, his enthusiasm withered when he found out he would have to go tandem. In other words, he wouldn't be allowed to jump out of the plane solo; he'd have to be tethered to the officer in case something malfunctioned. Call me crazy, but I'd far rather be tethered when free-falling from the sky!

In your life and mine lots of things can suddenly go wrong. In those moments, it might feel like we're free-falling. The great news is we're not flying solo. We are tethered to Jesus, who, in the words of the prophet Isaiah, is the "Wonderful Counselor, Mighty God, Everlasting Father, Prince of Peace" (Isaiah 9:6).

As believers, although we are tethered, we seem to have a hard time trusting that God won't let us fall. Learning to put our complete confidence in Jesus seems to give us pause. It sounds a little ethereal and passive, doesn't it? If we trust God, will we be able to relax, lay back, and simply coast through life? In reality, nothing could be further from the truth!

When challenging circumstances come, doubts often follow. We wonder, *Can I* actually *trust God? What does that even look like? Is He really good? Does He truly have my best interests in mind?*

I remember a season in my life when trusting God felt impossible. My community unraveled as we moved across the country. My health crumbled as I battled cancer and had multiple surgeries. My emotions came undone as I faced the abuse of my past. On top of all that, my husband's job collapsed. Everything I thought I believed about the Lord felt shaky. I felt as though God was no longer behaving like the God I thought I knew. During that season, I had a choice. Would I let go and walk away from my faith because I felt disappointed in God? Or would I choose to cling to what I knew of Christ's character though circumstances told me different?

I did choose to cling, although the most amazing thing to me is that even if I had let go, God would not have let me go! I was tethered by His goodness and the faithfulness of His promises.

Maybe you've not faced cancer or the loss of a job, but you've experienced other tragedies and have felt disappointed with God. Maybe you've lost a child. Maybe your marriage has fallen apart even though you prayed and did all you could to keep it together. Maybe you've been betrayed by a loved one. Maybe you've faced a financial crisis.

The looming question is, Can you trust God when life falls apart? How is it possible living in a broken world filled with disillusionment, heartache, disease, and violence? What does it look like to rely on God and relax in His goodness?

What we discover during those difficult seasons is that trust takes deliberate effort on our part. The psalmist gives us a starting point for our intentionality. He wrote, "Those who know your name trust in you, for you, Lord, have never forsaken those who seek you" (Psalm 9:10). In other words, if you want to have confidence and assurance in God, you must put a bit of effort into knowing His names. Why? His names reveal His character.

In this Girlfriend Gathering, we're going to look at four names of Christ that will give us amazing insight into His character and provide a firm tether for when the trials of life unfold.

Are you ready to get started?

Begin by opening your hands and praying, *Lord Jesus, I want to trust You. Open my heart to trust You more. Fill me with new insight into who You are and help me relax, knowing that your almighty character is fully good and sovereign.*

For to us a child is born,
to us a son is given,
and the government will be on his
shoulders.
And he will be called
Wonderful Counselor, Mighty God,
Everlasting Father, Prince of Peace.
—Isaiah 9:6

Session I

JESUS AS WONDERFUL COUNSELOR

When our son, J. J., was fourteen years old, I came home from a speaking event to discover that he had been vomiting all day. I felt concerned that he had the flu, but when he ate two pieces of strawberry pie that evening, I let go of my worries and figured it was a short-term stomach bug that had passed.

However, the next morning around 4:30 a.m., J. J. came into our bedroom doubled over in pain. After getting him back to bed, I got on my knees to beg God for wisdom. I didn't know what to do. It was a Sunday morning, which meant it would likely be impossible to get an appointment with our pediatrician. I wondered whether I should just wait until Monday during regular office hours. However, as I was praying, I felt the Holy Spirit prompt me to push to get J. J. seen right away. As it turned out, J. J. had appendicitis, and by the time they got him into surgery, his appendix had already burst. If I had waited much longer, it would have been life-threatening.

Honestly, that's just one example, but there have been so many times in my life when I have felt desperate for wisdom. I'm guessing it's the same for you. Probably just this past week there were moments when you felt unsure of the right path to take or the right decision to make. In those moments, we can turn to the Wonderful Counselor in prayer and cry out for wisdom.

To understand this a bit more, open your Bibles to the book of Isaiah.

Exploration

Read Isaiah 9:6 out loud.

The prophet Isaiah was writing approximately eight hundred years before Christ. At the time of his writing, the Assyrians were taking many Israelites into cruel captivity. It was a dark time in Israel's history. Isaiah's prophecy gave the people of God hope that a child would be born as the Messiah. He would come as the Savior. Though the religious leaders misunderstood this prophecy, Isaiah was speaking prophetically about Jesus Christ. "And he will be called Wonderful Counselor, Mighty God, Everlasting Father, Prince of Peace" (Isaiah 9:6). Though the prophecy was fulfilled through the birth of Jesus, it's ultimate fulfillment will be in the second coming of Christ.

Let's consider that first title, Wonderful Counselor. What does that mean?

As I've dug a bit deeper to discover the rich meaning behind the name Wonderful Counselor, I've gone back to the Hebrew. The Hebrew word for "wonderful counselor" is *pele-yovetz*. The first term, *pele*, means "wonder," which means something extraordinary or incomprehensible. The second term, *yovetz*, means "to advise, counsel."[1]

When you think of a great counselor, what characteristics come to your mind?

_____

_____

_____

_____

_____

_____

_____

_____

_____

_____

_____

_____

_____

_____

_____

_____

Read Romans 11:33–36.

The counsel that Christ brings to our lives defies our imaginations. His wisdom and understanding are beyond anything we can comprehend. After reading these verses, what adjectives would you use to describe Jesus's wisdom?

_____

_____

_____

_____

_____

_____

_____

_____

_____

_____

_____

_____

_____

_____

_____

Life-Changing Truths About Jesus as the Wonderful Counselor

Jesus has never-ending wisdom. Life is filled with unexpected twists and turns and countless decisions. Jesus's wisdom has no limits, and His judgments are always perfect. He was there at the beginning with the Father and came to show us the heart of the Father. As the Wonderful Counselor, He is the source of never-ending wisdom. His sovereign understanding is part of His nature and character. In other words, you cannot separate Him from His wisdom. The psalmist describes Him in this way, "Great is our Lord and mighty in power; his understanding has no limit" (Psalm 147:5). There are absolutely no boundaries on Jesus's understanding!

Jesus bends down with a listening ear. A counselor or coach listens and allows the client to process his or her thoughts and feelings. As the Wonderful Counselor, Jesus "bends down to listen" (Psalm 116:2 NLT). He hears and understands every whisper of our hearts. He not only listens to our prayers but also intercedes on our behalf before the Father (Romans 8:34).

So often my own thoughts are tangled. I feel conflicted or ambivalent as I consider the choices before me. When that happens, I know I need a private session with the Wonderful Counselor. I get on my knees and pour out my heart. Like the psalmists, I just dump all my conflicted feelings before the Lord. He listens to the cries of my heart, mends the fractures in my soul, and enables me to move forward on the right path. My heart echoes what the psalmist wrote, "I will praise the Lord, who counsels me; even at night my heart instructs me" (Psalm 16:7). When we pour out our hearts authentically, Jesus listens and shows us the path forward.

Jesus offers us His comforting presence. When our emotions are a mess or we feel confused, we long for empathy. Our hearts' desire is for someone to crawl into our sorrow with us and offer understanding. That is exactly what Jesus did and continues to do. He left the glory of heaven, entered our dirt and mess, and offered His own comforting presence. As the Wonderful Counselor, He continues to provide His understanding presence amid our chaos. The author of Hebrews reminds us that He understands and sympathizes with our every feeling (Hebrews 4:15). Just as in the Old Testament when God promised Moses that His presence would go with him (Exodus 33:14), so He promises us today that He will never leave us nor forsake us (Hebrews 13:5)—not when we're confused, not when we're doubting, and not when we're lonely.

Reflection

Group Reflection: Let's Get Real!

In this season of life, where are you most desperate for wisdom?

_____

_____

_____

_____

_____

_____

_____

_____

As friends how can you come alongside and support one another in your quest for wisdom?

_____

_____

_____

_____

_____

_____

_____

_____

_____

_____

_____

_____

_____

_____

_____

_____

At times, Jesus gives us wisdom through the voice of a friend, mentor, coach, or counselor. Have you ever had this experience where you felt God gave you the exact wisdom you needed through a human voice?

_____

_____

_____

_____

_____

_____

_____

_____

_____

_____

_____

_____

_____

_____

_____

_____

Have you ever participated in a Wisdom Council? (A Wisdom Council is when a group of people are gathered to help a specific individual discern what God is speaking.) If not, would that be something that excites you or intimidates you? Who would you include to be part of that?

_____

_____

_____

_____

_____

_____

_____

_____

_____

_____

_____

_____

_____

_____

How does knowing Jesus as the Wonderful Counselor help bolster your trust in Him?

_____

_____

_____

_____

_____

_____

_____

_____

_____

_____

_____

_____

_____

_____

Personal Consideration

When you feel desperate for wisdom, where do you most often turn first (for example, Google, a friend, husband)?

_____

_____

_____

_____

_____

_____

_____

_____

_____

_____

_____

_____

_____

How might your life look different if you went to God first?

_____

_____

_____

_____

_____

_____

_____

_____

_____

_____

_____

_____

_____

_____

Make a list of five people whom you consider to be both wise and Christlike whom you could go to for advice if you needed it.

_____

_____

_____

_____

_____

_____

_____

_____

_____

_____

_____

_____

_____

_____

_____

_____

Application

Invitation. Are there any action steps you feel like the Lord is inviting you to take as a result of studying Jesus as the Wonderful Counselor?

_____

_____

_____

_____

_____

_____

_____

_____

_____

_____

_____

_____

_____

Listen. Listen to "Perfect Wisdom of Our God" by Keith and Kristyn Getty.

Suggested Girlfriend Activities

- Visit an antique store and have each friend choose something small and cheap to remind her of the need for wisdom.

- Together, make a list of your favorite go-to passages when you feel the need for wisdom.

Prayer Time. Take turns praying over each other and asking Jesus to grant the wisdom that each friend needs. Keep a prayer journal as a group of friends where you can keep track of prayer requests and answers.

Practical Tips to Increase Your Wisdom

- Memorize Romans 11:33–36.

- When wrestling with a decision, keep a journal and write down any time you feel God speaks. After doing this for several weeks, look back on your journal and see if there are any patterns.

Additional Scripture Passages. Read these passages out loud over one another. Hearing the Word of God spoken out loud strengthens our faith.

The fear of the LORD is the beginning of wisdom;
    all who follow his precepts have good understanding.
    To him belongs eternal praise. (Psalm 111:10)

Get wisdom, get understanding;
    do not forget my words or turn away from them.
                        (Proverbs 4:5)

Walk with the wise and become wise,
    for a companion of fools suffers harm.
                         (Proverbs 13:20)

By wisdom a house is built,
    and through understanding it is established;
through knowledge its rooms are filled
    with rare and beautiful treasures. (Proverbs 24:3–4)

Be very careful, then, how you live—not as unwise but
as wise, making the most of every opportunity, because
the days are evil. (Ephesians 5:15–16)

Oh, the depth of the riches of the wisdom and knowledge
       of God!
    How unsearchable his judgments,
    and his paths beyond tracing out!
"Who has known the mind of the Lord?
    Or who has been his counselor?"
"Who has ever given to God,
    that God should repay them?"
For from him and through him and for him are all things.
    To him be the glory forever! Amen.
                        (Romans 11:33–36)

Blessing
Lord Jesus, we praise You that You are the Wonderful Counselor. You have infinite wisdom and understanding. Now, we bless one another. May we continually come to You to find wisdom. Thank You that we can trust You to answer us. May we walk as wise friends, making the most of every opportunity as we follow after Your heart.

Session 2

JESUS AS MIGHTY GOD

When I was a little girl, maybe eight or nine years old, I won a necklace at church. The necklace had a glass heart with a teeny, tiny mustard seed inside. I was told by the teacher that the mustard seed represented a tiny amount of faith. Jesus said, "Truly I tell you, if you have faith as small as a mustard seed, you can say to this mountain, 'Move from here to there,' and it will move. Nothing will be impossible for you" (Matthew 17:20–21).

Out of my back window, I have a glorious view of Pikes Peak. Three-quarters of the year the peak glistens with white snow. Standing in contrast to the vivid blue Colorado sky, it's an absolutely breathtaking view! As I look at that mountain daily, I often remember the necklace with the tiny mustard seed. I am reminded that the Mighty God who flung the stars in space can use the tiniest amount of faith that I have to do the impossible. Not because of my faith but because of His power as Mighty God.

There have been seasons in my life when I have felt desperate for the power of almighty God: when I walked through cancer, when the financial pressures were so great we didn't know if we'd survive, or when our children became ill and they desperately needed healing.

You have likely felt desperate for God's mighty power in your life as well. Perhaps your faith feels even tinier than a mustard seed. May I remind you? Circumstances might feel impossible, but Christ is the mighty God who says, "Nothing will be impossible."

Living in a chaotic world with mass shootings, global pandemics, threats of war, and economic uncertainty, we need the reminder that Jesus is the Mighty God. With anxiety, fear, and depression on the rise, we need to know that we are tethered to a God who is sovereignly in control. Nothing can separate us from His hold. We are held secure. Remembering that He is almighty God strengthens us to trust Him more.

Exploration

Read Isaiah 9:6 out loud.

What a beautiful prophetic picture of Jesus! Often, we celebrate this prophecy at Christmas, and we marvel that Christ came as an infant. We also need to remember that although He came as an infant, He came as Mighty God.

Asheritah Ciuciu writes so eloquently, "We do not trifle with a weakling, nor do we worship an incompetent wannabe rock star. We worship the King of kings who deserves all honor and glory, and continually receives it from the heavens, creation, angels, and the chorus of His redeemed."[1]

We need the reminder, don't we? In worshipping Jesus, we worship the Mighty God. Nothing can thwart His sovereign plans; nothing catches Him by surprise nor trips Him up. Nothing shakes Him or causes Him to lose His grip on us. He is the absolute Mighty One who firmly holds us in His hand.

As we think of Jesus as almighty God, several scenes come to mind. Let's look at each one. Have a different person read each of the following stories from the life of Jesus. Then reflect as a group on how the story demonstrates that Jesus is the Mighty God.

- Matthew 8:28–34
- John 9:1–11
- John 11:1–44

Life-Changing Truths About Jesus as the Mighty God

He holds on to us even if we let go. When my kids were little, my husband, Steve, loved taking them out into the waves when we were at the beach. At times, he would take them out pretty far, and honestly, I would cringe. Sometimes when the waves came crashing, little arms would let go of his neck; however, Steve's arms never let go. Their safety didn't depend on their ability to hold on to Steve; it depended on Steve's ability to hold on to them.

When I think of the challenges of life, often they feel like crashing waves. However, we are held secure by the Mighty One. At times we may doubt and stop clinging to Him, but He never lets go. In fact, the wind and the waves still obey His command. He is the one who continues to speak, "Peace! Be still!" (Mark 4:39 ESV).

His power is exceedingly abundantly beyond all you ask or think. His power is limitless. With Him nothing is impossible! Beyond that, when we are weak, His power is perfected in our weakness. As we learn to trust His power, we discover that all we need is provided for by Him.

Second Peter 1:3 assures us that "His divine power has given us everything we need for a godly life through our knowledge of him who called us by his own glory and goodness."

He transforms us by His Spirit. Jesus not only provides for us beyond what we are able to imagine but also transforms us by His Spirit. At different times in your spiritual journey, you may become discouraged, wondering, *Am I changing at all?* Rest assured, as you yield yourself to the Mighty God, He is changing you. He is transforming you by the power of His Spirit (Philippians 2:13).

He resurrects our broken dreams. All of us have had broken dreams, which left us feeling defeated and hopeless at times. But Jesus, as the Mighty God, is able to bring new dreams. He is the one who said, "I am the resurrection and the life" (John 11:25). When your dreams die, it's time for a resurrection!

Reflection

Group Reflection: Let's Get Real!

In recent months, have you experienced any set of circumstances that have felt impossible? Take turns sharing those situations. After each person shares, have one person in the group pray about those situations and invite almighty God to come into that situation with His power.

_____

_____

_____

_____

_____

_____

As you reflect on your life, where has Jesus shown Himself to be the Mighty One?

_____

_____

_____

_____

_____

_____

_____

_____

_____

_____

_____

_____

_____

_____

_____

How does remembering help strengthen your faith to trust Him more completely?

_____

_____

_____

_____

_____

_____

_____

_____

_____

_____

_____

_____

_____

_____

_____

Personal Consideration

What broken dreams have you experienced in your life? Where do you need Jesus to show up personally as almighty God to resurrect new life from what feels dead?

_____

_____

_____

_____

_____

_____

_____

_____

_____

_____

_____

_____

_____

_____

Describe a time in the space below where you experienced Jesus as Mighty God. Even if you already shared it with the group, journal about it in the space below because as you write about that situation, it will be planted in your memory and build your faith.

_____

_____

_____

_____

_____

_____

_____

_____

_____

_____

_____

_____

_____

Application

Invitation. As you've spent time reflecting on the power of almighty God, how do you feel He is inviting you to respond?

_____

_____

_____

_____

_____

_____

_____

_____

_____

_____

_____

_____

_____

_____

Listen. Listen to "Almighty God" sung by Passion, featuring Sean Curran.

Suggested Girlfriend Activities

- Gather around a fire if possible and get cozy. Talk about past answers to prayer you've experienced, fun activities you've done together, trials you've gone through together, and even funny experiences you've had together. Remembering together bonds you as friends and increases your faith. The following questions can help you get started:
    - What's the biggest answer to prayer you've seen as a group in the past two years?
    - What's the funniest experience you've had together in the past few years?
    - How have you celebrated one another's birthdays in the past year?
    - What's been one of the most meaningful conversations you've had with one another in the past year, and why was it significant?

- If possible, try doing a ropes course together. Afterward, process as a group what it looked like to conquer a ropes course. How did you have to trust one another as you did the course?

Practical Tips to Increase Your Trust in the Mighty God

- Pause and look back on God's faithfulness. Draw a timeline of your life and include times in your life when you experienced firsthand the power of almighty God. (For example, times when He restored a broken relationship, times when God allowed you to become pregnant despite struggling with infertility, or times when God unexpectedly provided for your financial needs.)
- Spend intentional moments worshipping God for His

almighty character. As we praise Him, the Holy One will increase our trust.

- At times when our trust feels like it's failing and our faith feels weak, we simply need to pray and ask the Holy Spirit to strengthen our trust in that moment.
- Foster a faith-filled community. God intends for us to live out our spiritual journeys in community. When your faith feels weak, dare to be real with a friend. Ask her to pray for you. Friends can carry us to the Father when we feel too weak to stand. As we lean into the stronger faith of another, our own faith is strengthened.

Additional Scripture Passages. Read these passages out loud over one another.

> LORD, the God of our ancestors, are you not the God who is in heaven? You rule over all the kingdoms of the nations. Power and might are in your hand, and no one can withstand you. (2 Chronicles 20:6)

> Jesus looked at them and said, "With man this is impossible, but with God all things are possible." (Matthew 19:26)

> Therefore God exalted him to the highest place
>   and gave him the name that is above every name,
> that at the name of Jesus every knee should bow,
>   in heaven and on earth and under the earth,
> and every tongue acknowledge that Jesus Christ is Lord,
>   to the glory of God the Father. (Philippians 2:9–11)

> Then I heard what sounded like a great multitude, like the roar of rushing waters and like loud peals of thunder, shouting:
>   "Hallelujah!
>   For our Lord God Almighty reigns."
>   (Revelation 19:6)

Blessing

Lord Jesus, we bow before You as the Mighty God. Thank You that nothing is too difficult for You! We bless one another. May we as a group of friends know and experience Your power in our lives. May our faith and trust grow as we pray for one another and watch how You, Lord, answer our prayers. Let us know beyond the shadow of a doubt that with You nothing is impossible!

_____

_____

_____

_____

_____

_____

_____

_____

_____

_____

_____

_____

_____

_____

_____

_____

_____

_____

_____

_____

_____

_____

_____

_____

_____

_____

_____

_____

_____

_____

_____

_____

_____

_____

_____

Session 3

JESUS AS EVERLASTING FATHER

When my kids were little there was a song they used to sing in Sunday school called "Father Abraham."[1] Maybe you know it? The song begins, "Father Abraham had many sons, many sons had Father Abraham." While they sang, the kids would swing first their right arms, then their left arms, then their right feet, and then their left feet. I'm not completely sure of the point of the song other than it was a great song to get wiggles out!

In Jewish culture, Abraham was considered the father of the faith. He was elevated and esteemed as being the patriarch of the nation Israel. Isaiah, however, prophesied that a child would be born, and as the Messiah, He would be the Father to the children of Israel. He would protect and provide for them, and His provision would not be limited by death but would go on through all eternity.

Jesus came as that Messiah, and while He came to reveal the heart of the Father, He also came as the Everlasting Father—the One who would be the Father of our faith. He would be the ultimate provider and protector of our salvation.

One day, Jesus got into a huge debate with the religious leaders around the topic of Father Abraham. For us, understanding the argument is a pivotal piece of understanding Jesus as the Everlasting Father. Let's take a look.

Exploration

Read John 8:31–58 out loud.

The debate began when Jesus instructed, "If you hold to my teaching, you are really my disciples. Then you will know the truth, and the truth will set you free" (John 8:31–32). The leaders argued back that they were descendants of Abraham and that they had never been enslaved by anyone.

Read Exodus 1:8–14.

Why was it a silly argument that they had not been enslaved?

_____

_____

_____

_____

_____

_____

_____

Jesus's point was that they were slaves to sin. However, the religious leaders kept returning to the fact that Abraham was their father (John 8:39). Why do you think this was so important to them?

_____

_____

_____

_____

_____

_____

_____

_____

_____

_____

_____

_____

_____

_____

_____

When Jesus stood and announced, "Before Abraham was born, I am!" (John 8:58), there was a collective gasp! In one fell swoop, Jesus had managed to tick off every single one of the religious leaders present. Why? Because Jesus was saying that from all eternity He was. In other words, He was claiming to be God, the God of Abraham, Isaac, and Jacob.

Read John 10:30.

In this passage what does Jesus assert?

_____

_____

_____

_____

_____

_____

_____

_____

_____

_____

_____

_____

In some ways the claim that Jesus would come as the Everlasting Father can feel confusing. God exists in three persons: God the Father, God the Son (Jesus Christ), and God the Holy Spirit. When the prophet Isaiah claimed that the Messiah would be known as the Everlasting Father, he was not diminishing the Trinity. He was showing us that, first and foremost, the Messiah is one with the Father and that from all eternity He was and is. Jesus is the Alpha and the Omega. Before the creation of the world, before any great historical event, Jesus existed with God the Father. He is the Father of our new creation as children of God.

As we think about Jesus being our Everlasting Father, our trust increases.

Life-Changing Truths About Jesus as the Everlasting Father

You can trust His love forever. From eternity to eternity, Jesus loves you. His love never shifts or wanes. No matter how rich and deep human love is, it will disappoint us from time to time. As our Everlasting Father, Jesus's love is perfect. It is constant and eternal. The psalmist reminds us in Psalm 136 with the refrain that "His love endures forever." Friend, you can do nothing today to make Him love you more or less.

You can trust Him to provide and protect. Fathers are supposed to provide for their families. Yet so many earthly fathers fall short. They are either unable or unwilling to provide. As the Everlasting Father, Jesus's provision is perfect. He provides the way to an intimate relationship with the Father. He provides for every need we have because He Himself is the Bread of Life (John 6:35). The apostle Paul promised us that Jesus would supply all our needs according to His riches (Philippians 4:19). In his letter to the Corinthians, Paul wrote, "And God is able to bless you abundantly, so that in all things at all times, having all that you need, you will abound in every good work" (2 Corinthians 9:8). All that you

45

need is wrapped up in Jesus. As the Everlasting Father, He is the perfect provider.

You can trust His timing in all things. Jesus holds a different perspective on forever. He sees the beginning and the end. As the Everlasting Father, He is also the Alpha and Omega. What do I mean? Alpha and omega are the first and last letters of the Greek alphabet. Jesus existed before all creation, and He will exist eternally as the never-ending One. He doesn't need a Google calendar or an Apple watch. He is not bound by time in any way, shape, or form. As such, He sees all of eternity and moves according to what is best for His purposes and your well-being. At times when we are waiting, it feels like God is terribly slow. However, His timing is perfect, and we can trust His timing in all areas of life.

You can trust Him to complete what He started in you. The apostle Paul wrote about Jesus, "For in him all things were created: things in heaven and on earth, visible and invisible, whether thrones or powers or rulers or authorities; all things have been created through him and for him" (Colossians 1:16). Just as He was the Father of your creation the first time, so He is the perfector of your faith. You can trust Him to continue the process of transformation in your life.

Reflection

Group Reflection: Let's Get Real!

Does it feel confusing to you that Jesus is called the Everlasting Father when He mentions God the Father often throughout the Gospels? Why or why not?

_____

_____

_____

_____

_____

_____

_____

_____

_____

_____

_____

_____

_____

_____

When you think of Jesus as the perfect provider, how have you been encouraged by His provision? Have you ever felt disappointed in His provision? How did you find peace amid your disappointment?

_____

_____

_____

_____

_____

_____

_____

_____

_____

_____

_____

_____

_____

_____

Jesus is the Father of our transformation, and the Holy Spirit fuels our transformation; yet we must cooperate and at times take active steps. What do you think is our part, and what do you think is His part?

_____

_____

_____

_____

_____

_____

_____

_____

_____

_____

_____

_____

_____

As the Everlasting Father, Jesus holds eternity in His hands. He knows the beginning from the end and holds a different perspective of time. In contrast, as humans, we are impatient people. When have you had a hard time waiting? How does knowing Jesus as the Everlasting Father change your view of waiting?

_____

_____

_____

_____

_____

_____

_____

_____

_____

_____

_____

_____

_____

_____

_____

Personal Consideration

As you reflect on Jesus as the Everlasting Father, what emotions are stirred in you?

_____

_____

_____

_____

_____

_____

_____

_____

_____

_____

_____

_____

_____

_____

Think about a specific time when you experienced Jesus providing for and protecting you. How does that help you trust Him in the future?

_____

_____

_____

_____

_____

_____

_____

_____

_____

_____

_____

_____

_____

_____

How has Jesus used seasons of delay in your life in the past? What have those seasons taught you about trusting His timing?

_____

_____

_____

_____

_____

_____

_____

_____

_____

_____

_____

_____

_____

_____

_____

Is there something specific you are waiting for in this season? Write a prayer expressing your desire to the Lord in the space below.

_____

_____

_____

_____

_____

_____

_____

_____

_____

_____

_____

_____

_____

_____

_____

_____

Application

Invitation. What do you feel God is inviting you to do as a result of knowing Him as the Everlasting Father?

_____

_____

_____

_____

_____

_____

_____

_____

_____

_____

_____

_____

_____

_____

Listen. Listen to "His Name Is Jesus" sung by Jeremy Riddle.

Suggested Girlfriend Activities

- Try baking a new recipe together. After it is finished enjoy your food together and spend some time reflecting on Christ's provision in your lives.
- Read Ephesians 6:10–17 and discuss how Christ is represented in each piece of the armor of God.
- Take a self-defense class together and reflect on how Jesus is our ultimate protector.

Practical Tips to Trust Jesus as the Everlasting Father

- Compare your earthly father to your Everlasting Father. Write down the differences, and then write out a prayer praising Jesus for revealing God the Father to you.
- Read through Luke 15. Write down the characteristics you see in Jesus that show you what God the Father is like.
- The next time you're in a season of waiting and tempted to doubt God's goodness, remind yourself that Jesus holds eternity in His hands. He sees the beginning from the end. He knows the exact right time to answer your prayer.

Additional Scripture Passages

The Son is the image of the invisible God, the firstborn over all creation. For in him all things were created: things in heaven and on earth, visible and invisible, whether thrones or powers or rulers or authorities; all things have been created through him and for him. He is before all things, and in him all things hold together. (Colossians 1:15–17)

Because Jesus lives forever. (Hebrews 7:24)

"I am the Alpha and the Omega," says the Lord God, "who is, and who was, and who is to come, the Almighty." (Revelation 1:8)

I am the Living One; I was dead, and now look, I am alive for ever and ever! And I hold the keys of death and Hades. (Revelation 1:18)

Blessing

Lord Jesus, Everlasting Father, I pray that You would bless us as friends. Help us sink more deeply into Your everlasting love. May we grow in our trust, understanding that You will never leave us or forsake us. Fill us with renewed faith as we rest in the knowledge that You are good, and Your love is everlasting.

_____

_____

_____

_____

_____

_____

_____

_____

_____

_____

_____

_____

_____

_____

_____

_____

_____

Session 4

JESUS AS PRINCE
OF PEACE

Hurricane Irma came barreling toward the coast of Florida as a category-four storm in August 2017. My husband, Steve, and I were at the Momentum Conference in Orlando. The conference started recommending that folks leave. Everyone was evacuating Florida. Meanwhile, our daughter Keri and her husband, Zach, were moving from Florida. With the hurricane coming fast, Zach left with the moving truck. Keri and her two little ones (two years and three months) drove to Orlando to meet Steve and me so that Keri and I could fly together to escape the impending storm.

When we arrived at the airport, chaos ensued. The lines were ridiculously long. I remember waiting in hot lines trying to entertain the two-year-old and hoping we were going to get on a flight in time. We did manage to get a flight and were some of the last to leave Florida. As a souvenir from the conference, I have a T-shirt that says, "I Survived Momentum 2017 #Irmagosh." It's one of my absolute favorites!

Storms in life can churn up chaos quickly and rob us of peace. Not just literal storms, like hurricanes, but personal storms like illness, an unexpected diagnosis, divorce, or financial stress can create havoc in our souls.

Jesus came to bring us peace. He not only orchestrated peace between us and God the Father but also promises to bring calm to the chaos of our lives. The prophet Isaiah foretold that the Messiah would come as the "Prince of Peace." Of the four names, this one is my favorite. Let's take a look.

Exploration

Read Isaiah 9:6.

As you think about the political and social unrest of the last few years, how might Jesus being the Prince of Peace affect our culture? What do you think is our responsibility in demonstrating His peace to the world?

_____

_____

_____

_____

_____

_____

_____

Read Romans 5:1.

What does it mean to you, personally, that Jesus gives us peace with God the Father?

_____

_____

_____

_____

_____

_____

_____

_____

_____

_____

_____

_____

_____

_____

Life-Changing Truths About Jesus as the Prince of Peace

When I think of Jesus being the Prince of Peace, three scenes come to mind:

I see Jesus calming the wind and waves with one rebuke (Mark 4:35–41). Jesus speaks and instantly the sea becomes quiet and still. I am reminded that, as the Prince of Peace, He can calm the storms in my heart with just a word. He is able to bring every tumultuous wave of worry to placid stillness.

Have each friend share what this story teaches you about Jesus as the Prince of Peace.

_____

_____

_____

_____

_____

_____

_____

_____

_____

_____

I see Jesus sitting by himself quietly enjoying the Father's presence (Mark 1:35–39). Although the disciples are putting pressure on Jesus to get moving, Jesus doesn't overexplain or become defensive. He doesn't get frazzled. He doesn't allow the expectations of the disciples to drive His ministry. He simply says, "Let us go somewhere else—to the nearby villages—so I can preach there also. That is why I have come" (Mark 1:38). I love this picture of Jesus. At times, the expectations of others make us feel stressed. Here's the thing: when I feel tense or frantic, I need to call upon the Prince of Peace who is willing and able to remind me that I need to be driven by His voice alone. He quiets my anxiety with His presence as I lean into Him.

Discuss as a group how the expectations of others can rob you of your peace.

_____

_____

_____

_____

_____

_____

_____

_____

_____

_____

I see Jesus inviting His tired followers to "Come with me by yourselves to a quiet place and get some rest" (Mark 6:31). Ah . . . doesn't that sound nice? Quiet place. Rest. Just enjoying the Prince of Peace. The truth is sometimes we're our own worst enemy, and we allow ourselves to become so busy that we live on a continual adrenaline rush. There sits Jesus inviting, not scolding, simply inviting, "Come . . . by yourselves . . . get some rest."

What does Jesus's invitation to come and rest tell us about the peace He wants to offer us?

_____

_____

_____

_____

_____

_____

_____

_____

_____

_____

_____

_____

Reflection

Group Reflection: Let's Get Real!

How does our present culture war against us feeling peaceful?

_____

_____

_____

_____

_____

_____

_____

_____

_____

_____

_____

_____

_____

_____

Share with the group what it looks like for you personally to receive Jesus's invitation to receive rest and enjoy quiet. Do you think peace is possible in your life? Why or why not?

_____

_____

_____

_____

_____

_____

_____

_____

_____

_____

_____

_____

_____

_____

_____

Read Colossians 3:15.

What do you think it means in practical terms to "let the peace of Christ rule in your hearts"?

_____

_____

_____

_____

_____

_____

_____

_____

_____

_____

_____

_____

_____

_____

Discuss as friends what most often robs you of peace.

_____

_____

_____

_____

_____

_____

_____

_____

_____

_____

_____

_____

_____

_____

_____

What spiritual practices have been the most helpful to you in experiencing the Prince of Peace?

_____

_____

_____

_____

_____

_____

_____

_____

_____

_____

_____

_____

_____

_____

_____

_____

Personal Consideration

Think back on a time when you felt peace in the presence of God. Describe that time as best you can. What contributed to the peace you felt? Do you feel it's possible to experience that peace again?

_____

_____

_____

_____

_____

_____

_____

_____

_____

_____

_____

_____

_____

_____

Application

Invitation. Are there any areas of life that you feel the Prince of Peace is wanting you to invite Him into?

_____

_____

_____

_____

_____

_____

_____

_____

_____

_____

_____

_____

_____

_____

_____

_____

_____

Listen. Listen to "Peace Be Still" by Hope Darst.

Suggested Girlfriend Activities

- Take a walk through a park or wildlife sanctuary and listen for the sounds of creation. Talk together about how the beauty of creation can help us experience the presence of the Prince of Peace.
- Sit in silence for two minutes as a group. Then share whether or not silence is hard for you. Why or why not? How does noise at times rob us from experiencing the peace Christ offers?

Prayer Time. Take turns praying over each other and ask that each friend would experience the peace that passes understanding. Pray that the Holy Spirit would calm the chaos in one another's lives and usher in peace instead.

Practical Tips to Experience Peace

- Practice sitting in silence daily. Try to completely relax in Christ's presence.
- Pause throughout your day and remind yourself that the Prince of Peace is with you. Pausing throughout your day is so helpful for experiencing the peace Christ offers. Slow down.
- Practice Spiritual Breathing. Exhale stress and imagine yourself inhaling the power of the Holy Spirit. This ancient practice came from Isaac Penington (1617–1680) who taught the church to wait for the leading of the Holy Spirit.[1]

Additional Scripture Passages

You will keep in perfect peace
  those whose minds are steadfast,
  because they trust in you. (Isaiah 26:3)

In peace I will lie down and sleep,
    for you alone, LORD,
    make me dwell in safety. (Psalm 4:8)

Blessed are the peacemakers,
    for they will be called children of God.
                             (Matthew 5:9)

I have told you these things, so that in me you may
have peace. In this world you will have trouble. But take
heart! I have overcome the world. (John 16:33)

Let the peace of Christ rule in your hearts, since as
members of one body you were called to peace.
                             (Colossians 3:15)

Blessing

Prince of Peace, we confess that often worry, stress, and anxiety flood our souls. Wrap us in Your peace today. May we be blessed with a sense of Your calm. May tension be replaced with tranquility. Hush the inner hurry that so often takes us captive and instead help us be still enough to hear Your voice. Lord, may we experience peace beyond human understanding. May we know the presence of Christ within and may we joyfully rest in You.

DECLARATION
OF TRUST

A s friends, you can proclaim this declaration of trust out loud
together. What we declare out loud, we often have an easier
time believing.

Lord, I trust You as my Wonderful Counselor.
You are the God of all wisdom, and I trust You to be my source
of wisdom.
I praise You that You invite me to come to You whenever
I lack discernment.
I believe that You will show me what to do.

Lord Jesus, I trust You as Mighty God.
I praise You that You are the One who hung the stars in place
and ordered the rotation of the planets.
I praise You that You are sovereignly in control.
You are powerful enough to move mountains and near enough
to hear every whisper of my heart.

Lord, I trust You as my Everlasting Father.
I praise You that from all eternity You are good.
Thank You for being the provider and
the protector of my salvation.

Thank You that because You are everlasting,
I can trust Your timing in all things.

Lord Jesus, I trust you as my Prince of Peace.
In a world full of chaos, thank You that
You are able to bring peace to my thoughts.
I trust You to calm my anxious heart and fill my mind
with peace.
Lord, I trust You.

SEVEN-DAY FOLLOW-UP DEVOTIONAL PLAN

On the following pages you will find a seven-day devotional plan to help you connect with God after your Girlfriend Gathering. I recommend that you stay in touch with one another and share your thoughts as you each complete the devotional plan. Choose what works best for you to be able to hear one another's thoughts and share your own. After a retreat or four-week Bible study ends, it can feel like a letdown. If you all commit to doing the follow-up devotional plan, you can keep the strong connections going.

Day I

LEAN

Trust in the LORD with all your heart,
    and lean not on your own understanding;
in all your ways submit to him,
    and he will make your paths straight.

—Proverbs 3:5–6

I don't know a single person who doesn't need wisdom, do you? We need wisdom in our relationships, our careers, our finances, and for all our decisions.

The writer of Proverbs wrote that the key to finding wisdom was to trust the Lord with all of our being. We are to *lean* into the Lord anytime we don't know what to do or how to proceed. Wisdom begins with Him. He is the Wonderful Counselor. What does this look like in your everyday life?

I believe it begins with a posture of prayer and seeking the Lord's wisdom in all areas of life. Our conversation with God is ultimately more important than the decision we end up making. When you ask God for wisdom, you put your faith in His promise to give wisdom to all those who ask. You rely on the truth that

His nature is absolute wisdom and that He desires to give you the discernment you need.

The next time you are wrestling with a decision, praise God that He will give you wisdom, and then ask boldly. Remember James wrote, "If any of you lacks wisdom, you should ask God, who gives generously to all without finding fault, and it will be given to you" (James 1:5).

Pause and Reflect

In what areas of life do you most often need wisdom? How has God shown you His wisdom in the past?

Respond to God's Invitation

God is inviting you to ask Him for wisdom. Start with prayer. Then try holding a Wisdom Council. Gather just a few close friends. Explain the area of your life where you need direction. Seek God in prayer together and then listen as a group for anything God might speak. Invite your friends to speak into the situation. If a friend feels the Lord spoke, listen but *always* test the message against Scripture. God will never speak anything contrary to His Word.

Pray

Lord Jesus, I praise You that You are the God of all wisdom. Thank You that You invite me to ask whenever I lack insight about what to do. Jesus, I desperately need wisdom in so many areas of my life. Fill me with Your Spirit, I pray, so that I might have discernment in all things. I pray that I would walk with wisdom today as I seek to live my life for You.

Listen

Listen to "Trust in God" sung by Elevation Worship.

Day 2

PLANT

But blessed is the one who trusts in the LORD,
whose confidence is in him.
They will be like a tree planted by the water
that sends out its roots by the stream.
It does not fear when heat comes;
its leaves are always green.
It has no worries in a year of drought
and never fails to bear fruit.

—Jeremiah 17:7–8

Recently, my friend Gayle's husband, Roger, had a heart attack in the middle of the night. After Roger was checked in at the ICU, Gayle said to me, "Becky, I was so calm, and really I shouldn't have been. It was the Lord for sure!" How true! Where does that type of peace come from? I believe it comes from spending time in the presence of God and allowing our roots to sink down deeply into His Word. That is exactly what Gayle has done for years. She has cultivated a life of trusting God by planting herself in the Word. As a result, when the heat came in the form of a heart attack, though she felt fearful, she was able to stay steady and strong.

That's the kind of trust I want to cultivate in my life. How about you?

Life is going to be filled with moments that are challenging and chaotic. Trials will come. You can count on them! However, when our faith is rooted in the character of God, we are bolstered by His strength. The prophet Jeremiah described this strength as having no "fear when heat comes" and "no worries in a year of drought" (Jeremiah 17:7–8). The psalmist wrote something similar in Psalm 1, when he said that those who meditate on God's Word will be like a tree planted by rivers of water. They will remain fruitful and strong in every season (Psalm 1:2–3).

Pause and Reflect

When crises hit your life, how do you normally respond? How might planting your faith deeply in the character of God help steady and strengthen you for the difficult seasons of life?

Respond to God's Invitation

You might be wondering in the thick of your busy life, how do you plant your life in God's Word? You might be thinking, *Becky, you don't get my life!* Friend, it's not like you have to spend hours reading your Bible. Instead, read a small portion every day and ask the Holy Spirit to awaken your heart to the character of God. Another great option is listening to Scripture through the Bible app. You can even listen while driving or doing dishes. A good place to start is the Gospel of Mark. It's filled with stories that reveal the character of Jesus. Why not read one small section per day and write down one truth about what you see in Jesus's character? Gradually, as you continue, your trust in God's goodness will grow.

Pray

Lord Jesus, I want to be like the person described in Jeremiah 17 who has no fear when the heat comes and no worries in times of drought. I want my confidence to be firmly rooted in Your holy character. Help me meditate on who Scripture says You are both day and night so that I am able to rest securely in You. Take me deeper, I pray, in trusting You.

Listen

Listen to "Tend" sung by Emmy Rose and Bethel Music.

Day 3

REMEMBER

I remember the days of long ago;
I meditate on all your works
and consider what your hands have done.

—Psalm 143:5

There are times in our lives when battles close in around us and trusting God feels impossible. Maybe God feels silent or distant. How do you trust Him then? The key is to remember!

Remember the goodness of the Lord and how He has worked in the past. By remembering often, we find the strength to trust God in the present situation. Moses instructed the Israelites, "Be careful that you do not forget the LORD, who brought you out of Egypt, out of the land of slavery" (Deuteronomy 6:12).

Remember times when you felt His presence. When the psalmist David was in the wilderness and likely having a hard time trusting God, he remembered, "I have seen you in the sanctuary and beheld your power and your glory" (Psalm 63:2).

Remember how His character has been your provision. When the people of God felt afraid while rebuilding the wall under Nehemiah's leadership, Nehemiah encouraged them, "Don't be afraid of them. Remember the Lord, who is great and awesome" (Nehemiah 4:14).

When we remember, trust becomes easier.

Pause and Reflect

Are you a sentimental person? Do you enjoy looking through old photos or remembering fun events in the past? How might your sentimentality help your faith walk?

Respond to God's Invitation

Think back over the past few years. In what ways have you seen God work either on your behalf or on behalf of your loved ones? Look through photos and spend time thanking the Lord for His faithfulness in the past. Ask Him for renewed grace to trust Him with tomorrow.

Pray

Lord Jesus, thank You for all the ways You have moved in my life in the past. Holy Spirit, in the times when life closes in, and I feel tempted to doubt Your goodness, help me remember. I praise You for all You have done in my life and for what You will continue to do.

Listen

Listen to "This Is Our God" sung by Phil Wickham.

Day 4

FIX

Fixing our eyes on Jesus, the pioneer and perfecter of faith.
—Hebrews 12:2

My husband, Steve, used to run track in high school. He was best at the shorter races and actually broke a few school records. His coach really liked Steve and taught him to keep his eyes on the finish line.

The same principle holds true in our journey to trust God. When the race of life gets hard, we need to lift our eyes to Jesus, who is at the finish line cheering us on. When we fix our eyes on Jesus, we have less chance of growing weary in our trust journey. The energy to continue will come from Him.

Similarly, the prophet Isaiah wrote,

> You will keep in perfect peace
>   those whose minds are steadfast,
>   because they trust in you. (Isaiah 26:3)

The key to a steadfast mind is where we focus our thinking. We are the only created beings who have the ability to direct our thoughts. When we direct them toward Jesus, two things happen. Our trust grows, and we experience peace.

How do we fix our eyes on Jesus? Here are just a few ideas:

- Spend a few moments of every day thanking Him for His gifts to you.
- Rehearse His character traits when you feel anxious.
- Talk with Him throughout the day.

Pause and Reflect

What most often distracts you from keeping your focus on Jesus? How do you think your trust might increase if your life was more focused on Him?

Respond to God's Invitation

What practices help keep your focus centered on Jesus? Are there any new habits you would like to put in place to help keep your eyes fixed on Him?

Pray

Lord Jesus, I praise You for being the author and finisher of my faith. I confess that so often I feel distracted by _____ *(fill in the blank with what most distracts you). Help me remember to focus on You today. I lift my eyes to You alone.*

Listen

Listen to "Turn Your Eyes" sung by The Belonging Co., featuring Natalie Grant.

Day 5

WAIT

Wait for the LORD;
  be strong and take heart
  and wait for the LORD.

—Psalm 27:14

I'm an impatient person by nature. I wish I wasn't, but I am. And, if there's any place that can stretch the patience of even the most patient person, it's the DMV. Go in to change your license and you could be there for hours. Right?! I remember years ago, going for the third time to the DMV in California to renew my license and arriving first thing in the morning so I would be near the front of the line for customer service. However, on this particular day as the line grew literally around the building waiting for them to open, I peeked in the window to see a clerk wearing bunny ears. It seemed the DMV had decided to have an employee Easter egg hunt before opening, which delayed the opening for an hour. Trust me when I say there were a lot of impatient people waiting that day!

Waiting is hard. It just is! However, in our spiritual journey, waiting is essential to building our trust in God. Jesus is known as the Alpha and Omega (Revelation 1:8). He holds time and eternity in His almighty hands. As the Everlasting Father, as we studied, He holds a completely different perspective on time. Therefore, it's important that we learn to wait because, while God is always on time in our lives, He is never in a hurry. If we are going to learn to trust His timing, we must learn to wait. That's where the rub comes for most of us. When we are waiting for God to answer our prayers, the temptation comes to doubt God's goodness. We wonder: If God is good, why isn't He answering my prayers?

Let me reassure you, God is answering your prayers, but perhaps not according to your timetable. And the time you spend waiting is not wasted. God uses the waiting periods in our lives to strengthen our faith and shape our character.

Pause and Reflect

We're all waiting in some area of our lives. How is God meeting you in your waiting?

Respond to God's Invitation

Scripture promises that those who wait on the Lord will renew their strength (Isaiah 41:10). As you wait on Him, God is inviting you to trust. What does this look like in your life?

Pray

Lord Jesus, I confess waiting is hard for me. Yet, I know that You are inviting me to grow in the realm of patient waiting and steadfast trust. Strengthen me, I pray, as I worship You and wait. May hope grow within me as I learn to trust You more completely.

Listen

Listen to "Take Courage" sung by Kristene DiMarco.

Day 6

HOPE

May the God of hope fill you with all joy and peace as you trust
in him, so that you may overflow with hope by the power
of the Holy Spirit.

—Romans 15:13

Hope isn't wishful thinking. Hope is looking forward to something happening based on reliable facts. It is the assurance of things not yet seen or realized that we believe will happen. And, hope is essential to trust.

The apostle Paul prayed that the believers living in Rome would be filled with joy, peace, and overflowing hope. Where does hope come from, and how do we get more of it when we feel like ours is dwindling? The Holy Spirit living and dwelling within pours hope into our hearts, but we have to cooperate. How do we do that?

We stay in the Scriptures to keep our faith grounded in the truth about God. We meditate on His character, His love, His goodness, and His faithfulness, and the Holy Spirit fills our hearts with hope.

The second way we keep hope alive is to remember how God has worked in the past. When life feels dark or God feels distant, it is helpful to remind ourselves of what He has already accomplished in our lives. This gives us the faith boost to trust Him with our futures. In psalm 77, Asaph felt discouraged until he remembered. He made an intentional choice to remember the goodness of the Lord so that his hope would be restored and his trust strengthened. He wrote, "I will remember the deeds of the LORD; yes, I will remember your miracles of long ago" (Psalm 77:11).

Pause and Reflect

Has there ever been a time in your life when you felt hopeless? What did you do to rekindle your hope? How did you see God move in that season?

Respond to God's Invitation

God wants us to live a life filled with joy, peace, and hope overflowing. What practices might you put in place to respond to God's invitation of hope?

Pray

Lord Jesus, I praise You that You promised me a life filled with hope. Holy Spirit, in the moments when I feel my hope slipping, would You rekindle expectation as I lean into You and remember the ways You've worked in the past? Fill me today with joy, peace, and increased hope as I continually look to You.

Listen

Listen to "You've Already Won" sung by Shane and Shane.

Day 7

PRAISE

Praise the LORD.
Praise the LORD, my soul.
I will praise the LORD all my life;
    I will sing praise to my God as long as I live.

—Psalm 146:1–2

The single practice that has most increased my trust in God has been learning to be intentional about praising Him. I learned this while journeying through cancer. Although walking through cancer was horrific, it was extremely clarifying in my life. As I intentionally praised God for who He was every day, I felt His presence in ways I had never experienced before, and my trust grew. You simply can't praise God authentically and not be changed. As we praise Him, the Holy Spirit increases our faith.

Why is praising God so vital to our trust? Here are just a few reasons.

Praising God allows us to experience His presence more fully. The psalmist wrote that God inhabits the praises of His people (Psalm 22:3 KJV). It's not that God moves closer. He's already closer than you could ever imagine. It's that as we praise God intentionally, the Holy Spirit awakens our senses to experience God's presence more deeply. As a result, we become overwhelmed with the immensity of the love of God.

Praising God silences the Enemy. The Enemy of our souls often targets us with doubts and fears, but he can't stand when we're praising God. As we praise God, Satan flees. The psalmist wrote,

> Through the praise of children and infants
> you have established a stronghold against your enemies,
> to silence the foe and the avenger. (Psalm 8:2)

Even the praise that comes from the lips of children shuts up the mouth of the Enemy.

Praising God breaks the chains of bondage in our lives. When Paul and Silas were in prison in Philippi, they sang hymns and praised God while in their chains. The other prisoners, fascinated, were listening. As they sang and praised God, an earthquake struck, the prison doors flew open, and their chains came off (Acts 16:25–40). What a beautiful illustration of the power of praise. As you choose to praise God above your circumstances, the chains of fear, shame, and guilt will break off you. Your trust in God will be strengthened, and you will walk in freedom.

Pause and Reflect

Why do you think praising God has such a powerful impact on our lives?

Respond to God's Invitation

Jesus is inviting you to start becoming intentional about praising Him. An easy way to begin is to start each morning by praising and thanking God for His love. In the evening before you drift off to sleep, praise Him for His faithfulness throughout the day. In addition, here are a few other ideas:

- Use your car time as praise time. Turn on worship music, and praise God while you drive.
- Take a worship walk and let the beauty of creation prompt your praise.
- Stop at lunchtime and praise God that He is the Bread of Life.
- When you feel worried, shift your focus to God's character and spend time praising Him for His attributes.

Pray

I exalt You, Lord Jesus! I praise You for Your unfailing love and faithfulness in my life. Your mercies are new every morning, and Your blessings are evident every evening. I worship You because You are holy, compassionate, and forgiving. Your presence surrounds me, and You promise You will never leave or forsake me. Thank You that You go before, behind, above, and beneath me as I move through my day. I am overwhelmed by Your goodness, Lord! I live to worship You.

Listen

Listen to "Praise" sung by Elevation Worship.

ACKNOWLEDGMENTS

No book is ever written without many people contributing. That is definitely the case with *Tethered Trust*. My thanks to:

My husband, Steve, for the many nights when I'm approaching a deadline and feel too spent to cook, so we go out to dinner. Thanks for hanging in there and giving me the space to finish. I love you!

To my daughter and amazing editor, Bethany Lindgren. Bethany, it is always a delight to work with you on a project. I am so blessed to have you not only as my daughter but also as my editor. I love you!

To my son-in-law Chris Lindgren for the many nights you spent with your five boys so Bethany could finish this project. I love you!

To my son, Josiah Harling, and daughter-in-law, Shaina, for allowing me to process ideas and helping me cultivate my love for writing. You both are incredibly encouraging. I love you both!

To my daughter Stefanie Holder and my son-in-law Dave, thanks for being wonderful and for the times you spent listening and helping me process. I love you both!

To my daughter Keri Denison and my son-in-law Zach. Thanks for checking in on the writing process and for being interested in my projects. I love you both!

To my amazing grandkids, Charlie, Ty, Josh, Selah, Zachary, Theo, Noah, Rayna, Cayden, Kinley, Tori, Melody, Asher, and Austin. You guys fill my heart with so much joy! I love you all and pray for you each to grow up to love and serve Jesus.

To my agent and treasured friend, Blythe Daniel. Thanks for believing in the ideas God lays on my heart and for always being a woman of prayer. I love you!

To all the men and women at Iron Stream Media. John Herring and Susan Cornell, thank you for believing in the Girlfriend Gathering series!

To my amazing interns, Tiffany Curtis and Lynsey L'Ecuyer. I love working with you both and am so thankful for all the help you give. You are both precious to me!

To the amazing women of New Life East. I love you and love serving you!

NOTES

Session 1: Jesus as Wonderful Counselor

1. "Isaiah 9:6," s.v., Wonderful Counselor, Bible Hub Lexicon, https:// biblehub.com/lexicon/isaiah/9-6.htm.

Session 2: Jesus as Mighty God

1. Asheritah Ciuciu, *Unwrapping the Names of Jesus: An Advent Devotional* (Chicago: Moody, 2017), 31.

Session 3: Jesus as Everlasting Father

1. Jacob Uitti, "Who Wrote the Traditional Campfire Song 'Father Abraham,'" American Songwriter, February 2023, https://americansongwriter .com/who-wrote-the-traditional-campfire-song-father-abraham/.

Session 4: Jesus as Prince of Peace

1. Isaac Penington, "Waiting for Breathings from His Spirit," in *Devotional Classics*, ed. Richard J. Foster and James Bryan Smith (San Francisco: HarperSanFrancisco, 1999, 2005), 207.

If you enjoyed this book, will you consider sharing the message with others?

Let us know your thoughts. You can let the author know by visiting or sharing a photo of the cover on our social media pages or leaving a review at a retailer's site. All of it helps us get the message out!

Email: info@ironstreammedia.com

  @ironstreammedia

Iron Stream, Iron Stream Fiction, Iron Stream Kids, Brookstone Publishing Group, and Life Bible Study are imprints of Iron Stream Media, which derives its name from Proverbs 27:17, "As iron sharpens iron, so one person sharpens another." This sharpening describes the process of discipleship, one to another. With this in mind, Iron Stream Media provides a variety of solutions for churches, ministry leaders, and nonprofits ranging from in-depth Bible study curriculum and Christian book publishing to custom publishing and consultative services.

For more information on ISM and its imprints, please visit
IronStreamMedia.com